Trave

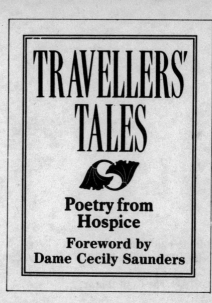

TRAVELLERS' TALES

Poetry from Hospice

Foreword by
Dame Cecily Saunders

Edited by Jane Eisenhauer

Marshall Pickering

Marshall Morgan and Scott
34–42 Cleveland Street, London W1P 5FB, U.K.

First published in 1989 by Marshall Morgan and Scott
Publications Ltd
Part of the Marshall Pickering Holdings Group

British Library Cataloguing in Publication Data
Travellers' Tales. Poetry from Hospices.
  I. Eisenhauer, Jane
  821′.914′08

  ISBN 0-551-01958-1

Set in Times by Avocet Robinson, Buckingham
Printed in Great Britain by Cox & Wyman Ltd, Reading,
Berks.

FOREWORD

When in crisis we move fast and many of us have seen people live a lifetime in a few weeks; facing old fears and finding them lose their power; accepting loss and finding it turn to growth. These poems have the same urgency about them; a few words sum up an overwhelming emotion, and symbols and pictures hold deep and sometimes surprising thoughts.

In their honesty they are not all peaceful or triumphant. Questions hang in the air or answers are bleak and desolate. Life and death are being faced in often stark reality.

Hospice life is like that, a patchwork of very different feelings. Visitors frequently remark on the atmosphere of peace and of freedom from pain but it is often peace in the eye of the storm and all the stronger for that. For those who go on looking, there is one important exploration to make − people are still themselves, perhaps themselves more than ever, and there are still new discoveries being made.

Poetry workshops, or individual encouragement to write, can be an important part of this hospice journey. A way in which those cared for and those caring can reach the place where they can say, as it were, 'I'm me, and somehow, that is all right.' Like their poems, hospice patients help us to meet and celebrate that truth.

Cicely Saunders
London, 1989

The editor acknowledges with grateful thanks the help of the writers, their families and the following hospices in the compilation of this anthology:

Cynthia Spencer House, Northampton, Northants.
Farleigh, Chelmsford Hospice, Chelmsford, Essex.
Katharine House Hospice Trust, Banbury, Oxon.
St. Christopher's Hospice, Sydenham, London SE26.
St. Francis House, Berkhamstead, Herts.
St. Helena's Hospice, Colchester, Essex.
St. John's Hospice, Lancaster, Lancs.
St. Joseph's Hospice, Hackney, London E8.
St. Luke's Hospice, Plymouth, Devon.
St. Luke's Nursing Home, Sheffield, South Yorks.
Strathcarron Hospice, Stirlingshire.
Ty Olwen, Swansea, West Glamorgan.

All royalties to go to the charity 'Help the Hospice'.

PREFACE

An anthology of poetry from hospice begs at least one question — for those not already involved there needs to be some explanation as to what hospice is. Basically, it is a philosophy as opposed to a particular type of building. The present-day hospice, as distinct from the original hospice which provided rest for travellers, is usually concerned with the care of those with a life-threatening illness which has reached a stage where it is no longer appropriate to continue to adopt specific curative treatment. Hospice seeks to meet all the needs of these people and their families, be they medical, nursing, social, psychological or spiritual. The emphasis is on 'quality of life', and recently it has been felt that the Arts should be an integral part of this frame. My interest is in the role that literature in general and poetry in particular can play.

Through research undertaken from 1985 to 1987, based at St. Joseph's Hospice in Hackney and funded by The Sir Halley Stewart Trust, I became aware that my fascination in the link between poetry and hospice care was not entirely spurious nor idiosyncratic. Not only did the reading of poetry bring comfort and excite interest but a surprising number of the people involved, either professionally or personally, were writing poems about their experiences and emotions.

Hospices that I visited, to talk about poetry and literature, all had one or two poems that were important to them.

Once it was known that the poems were 'out there', the Arts Executive Committee of the charity Help the Hospices sent out a circular asking for poems written in hospices to be sent to me so that this work could be considered for publication. Slowly the poetry came in.

By 1988 the publishers Marshall Pickering felt that the poems that had been collected constituted a viable publishing concern. So *Travellers' Tales* was born and a new impetus given to the collation of the poetry. Gradually more work from relatives, doctors, nurses, and others concerned in the provision of care started to appear alongside those written by patients.

But was it poetry? To define poetry has much exercised the academic mind and I have neither inclination nor perhaps the wit to enter the debate here. If someone told me they had written a poem and it was not obviously a sonata or a novel then who was I to argue? Certainly the poems here belong to no one particular school or tradition but they all contain the trace elements of what I believe to be poetry — metaphor, imagery, symbolism, meter and sometimes obvious rhyme.

As the poems here are only a very few of those that I have received over the past years, there has of course been a degree of subjective evaluation. I do not actually like some of the poems very much, but have tried to be as objective as possible by maintaining that the criterion for inclusion, quite apart from being relevant, is simply that the poem should be able to stand alone without biographical detail or explanation. Many poems are precious only to the writers and those close to them and so would have needed careful labelling before being exposed to those unaware of the circumstances in which they were written. The poems here are, I believe, mature enough to sink or swim on their own merit.

When such a personal, sensitive and painful world is exposed there are obvious inherent dangers. Quite rightly one can be accused of sensationalism, exploitation or mawkish bad taste. I hope I have managed to avoid the more obvious pitfalls. Permission has been given for all the poems that appear here to be published either by the writer or their families, except for those few marked 'anonymous', which were simply sent to me. I have chosen to believe that the very act of sending implied consent.

This anthology is not meant to be 'The Voice of Hospice' for this country of exploration is not peopled by some homogeneous group. Two important aspects of hospice — humour and despair — do not translate easily one often too fleeting and the other too deep for simple crafting. But poems ranging from the starkly simple *Girls*:

> There was Kay
> From Golders Green
> and several
> in between
>
> Now there's nothing.

to the more optimistic message of *The Challenge*:

> . . . For to live is the challenge — for me, for me
>   To battle my way through each day
> Determined that each day, a bonus shall be,
>   In a strange and a different way . . .

give some idea of the various concerns of those involved. Often it is clear from the poems that the person in receipt of care is the expert on what is needed to sustain the travel. Those providing the care are the 'sherpas' — there to carry the luggage, offer a helping hand over the uneven ground, occasionally give advice and provide relief from the physical distress of the long journey.

There are certainly more stories to be told. Those that appear here are just a few of the ones of which I am aware.

Jane Eisenhauer
London, 1989

KNOW THIS NOW

If I should leave
and the leaving unexpected,
with no time for any look or word;
then know this now,
that all has been said that could be said between us;
we are not cheated by words
that from necessity went unheard.

All partings come
unexpected or expected,
if in one or a hundred years;
but those unavowed links of love are not broken,
so true are the words we have spoken:
Eternity is ours, and, unwelcome death
know this now.
For us you hold no fears.

Grace Smith

THE GUEST

Today he came into the house.
   On coming round
   from one of my dizzy spells
I found him there.

To be perfectly honest
   it wasn't a complete surprise.
   He'd been dropping hints
for months.

But what with the W.I. . . .
   and The Wedding . . .
   I tried to ignore . . .
Believed it would go away.

But now with him
   sitting beside me,
   Death is no longer a stranger.
He has entered my door.

I do not know how to behave.
   I have not been educated
   to entertain this guest.
I have so much to learn.

V.G. Stevens

TAKE-OVER

Time was, I ruled, mistress in my own world.
My children and my dogs
acknowledged me as the centre of their lives.
I gave them love and they returned it;
I recognised their right to their own will
as they recognised mine.
My husband stood then, as now, on the periphery of my
dreams.

Now much has changed.
My body houses an unwelcome guest
who invites curiosity
and demands to be noticed.
Doctors and nurses dance attendance on him.
I will hold him in check with love and fierce will,
but he returns nothing, seeking only to invade further
his territory.

His insistence engages me in daily battles;
He fosters fears and seeks domination at my expense;
Already he has forced me from my home.
I wander rootless.
I shall not give up
'I think, therefore I am'.
So when I meet you, doctors, nurses, sister, daughter,
friends,
Concentrate your thoughts on me
not on this invader.
I remain mistress of myself.

Hazel Hampton

THE SECRET

We have a secret, shared by all yet known by few.
Our secret, more certain for us privileged few.
Yet as before, by minions, still undecided.
They desire, but do not need, to share the secret with us.
For there he stands, unseen in form.
Hidden by black or silver-edged clouds of luminosity,
The tool of his trade, his speciality,
Gleaming bright as a myriad of stars.
Sparkling keenly in our evening air.
Ashen handle held by shielded, gnarled hands
Ready at a second's bidding to
Flash out once or a thousand times.
Catching our secret from our innermost minds,
Blinding it with so many others
Into oblivion, from whence we came
And will return.

Jack Donoghue

CAN YOU DROWN IN THE STYX?

I wonder how deep The Styx is.
Can you paddle, wade or swim across?
Or are you obliged to take the ferry.

And suppose you haven't got the fare —
Do you wait for eternity on one side,
Continually wondering what's on
the other?

Jack Donoghue

TOO SOON

Bad news
  happens too soon.

Good news
  seldom occurs of its own volition!

Bad news
  switches itself on and off

With a bias
  in the direction of the bad.

Difficult to switch on
  being good —

I'm switched on
  in neutral.

That means the senses
are left in the passive.

So I am neither good nor bad;
black nor white.

I am a zebra.

Fred Julian

MY WAY TO SURVIVE BIG C

All gone, more tomorrow,
Find the praise
Die for sorrow
Say a wording
In a day.

Name the price
Your own way.

Don't give false hope,
'Cept your own
Goals, objectives,
Where to go.

I plan destiny
With open eye,
To take right out
The burdening sigh.

Adam Moffat

TO J. ALFRED PRUFROCK

There will be no time. There will not.
There will be no time. No.

No time for decisions or indecisions
or visions or revisions, to linger or
walk in-and-out the door; to prepare a smile
or to ask 'what is it?'

No time to crumple a bed, settle a pillow
or presume that it was (or was not) worth it;
no time for mellow October, to ponder, create
or to wonder 'shall I grow old?'

The silent clock drowns the seconds
It will not disturb the Universe,
the eternal footman holds the Truth.
I ask him no question, I am not afraid.

Grace Smith

THE QUESTION

Why should it happen to you? they say.
  Why should it happen to you?
Why should life come to a standstill,
  With no hope of dreams to survey?
Nothing to look for but pain or despair.
  How can you live life this way?

The answer is simple and clear in my mind.
  For the compensations are great,
And far outweigh the traumas of life
  Which avalanche daily, combined
To precipate pain and despair.
  So where is the secret confined?

The secret lies in discovering worth,
  Through others' reactions and feelings;
Through caring and sharing and healing.
  One is learning of love since the moment of birth,
And the mind can respond where the body cannot
  To find God's peace on this earth.

Liz Selby

WHAT'S IT ALL ABOUT?

What's it all about, this time we spend on Earth,
  to send but ripples in life's pond or round
    to touch those we love or know within our net —
    or someone who wanders in,
       then like smoke fades away.
        They go forgotten like a song,
          No more than a vague memory.

For a moment we touch
and are connected in a common bond
before, redirected along different paths
where priorities dictate, we shall not meet
but become as ghosts within the night.

But we all need someone to share our burden
  That special one that doesn't fade.
    To whom we cling knowing the support is not as smoke
    To give the drive through life's maze
       a purpose and a reason, before we too drift
       forgotten, but to a few,
         to just a ripple on the pond.

Bill Ellis

DO AS YOU WERE BEFORE

Float cool as ice slide down by the river
Dreams sunshine hot merge your brain;
The thoughts you have inside you are a dangerous vision,
A suicide murder in the old school yard.

Do you dream so when you weren't there —
The thoughts of illusion,
A man in despair
Why did I sell thee in secret mission
Unknown to succeed Vendata — persona non grata.

Indigenous thoughts lead to scary ways —
Ways of the wide one
In terminal care;
Follow his footsteps, but don't cross the bridge,
Cross down to the water thinking in ridge.
Dreams of a thought you left behind.
Minds entwined but never find.

Complexities nervosa
The ultimate in crime.

Adam Moffat

WHERE ARE MY FRIENDS?

When I was strong
   and full of laughter,
      They never left me.

When I was rich
   and giving generously,
      They came courting.

When I was climbing up
   up and away,
      They were beside me.

When they called out
   in the night,
      I went visiting.

When they fell,
   and needed a helping hand,
      I helped.

When they asked
   for love,
      I gave myself.

Now I am suffering and bitter.
   Now I am in need.
      Now I am abandoned.

Anonymous

AFRAID

I am afraid of death;
      death rather than dying;
fear of the unknown.

Nothing is worse than death.

Life is terribly important.
      any sort of life —
just being alive . . .

Life is important even if
      the importance of life
is sometimes hidden . . .

Life is important because,
      I am afraid of death.

Fred Julian

SOLITUDE

I walk alone
across an endless, darkened plain.
Its silent space
reflects the numbing sadness of my heart,
emptied of expectation.

But as I go
the darkness is no longer void;
Other footsteps, many sighs, are joined to mine.

They tell me I belong
to the vast and shabby company
of the bereft.
Within that kinship
peace begins to fill my heart.

Now as we journey
the wilderness and solitary place
are suddenly made glad.
For God Himself is one with us.
He is our Ransom and our Recompense.
This way is His
and leads us, singing, home to Zion.

Cicely Saunders

FAITH, HOPE AND TRUST

Hope   is the land I walk oh Lord

Trust   is the hill I scaled − Calvary's shrine.

Faith   is the greatest task you gave me dear Lord
        A great big, tall mountain to climb.

Ben Jackson

THE CHALLENGE

Life is a challenge − 'tis said, 'tis said.
    Life is a challenge to all.
A challenge encompassing everyone's days,
    Whether we rise or fall.

What is my challenge? − I ask, I ask.
    Now that my sickness has come.
Others are coping and caring and tending.
    Has a new era begun?

I'm no longer able − to fight, to fight.
    To reach for a goal to achieve.
No more do I feel that sense of attainment
    Through which the hours used to weave.

Life's still a challenge — I know, I know.
  But the challenge has changed.
Priorities being the people I meet
  With relationships rearranged.

My body is frail — I know, I know.
  But still I have much to give.
I shall use every muscle and fibre and tissue,
  On each of the days that I live.

For to live is the challenge — for me, for me.
  To battle my way through each day.
Determined that each day, a bonus shall be,
  In a strange and a different way.

To offer to others — my life, my life.
  And to share with them pleasure and pain.
Oh, may I succeed in my challenge in life,
  Until death shall reach out once again.

Liz Selby

THE HOSPICE

See the gates they beckon me
Won't you come inside.
I'll give you my protection
Within me you can hide.

There's no need to explain
The reason you are here.
I'll close my gates around you
And lock out all your fear.

So come when peace is what you seek,
With what little faith you have,
You know if it's to God you speak
He'll lend to you his staff.

Eileen Tompkins

STARTING POINT

Only forty years old —
No one to leave,
Nothing done for good or ill
For the world to remember.
A leaf floats down the river
And is lost forever,
No trace left behind.

Someone comes to listen
I find I have something to say.
I remember — a child in Warsaw —
The Rabbi, my grandfather,
Calls me down from bed,
Makes me talk far into the night,
Search out the ways of God.

Somehow
In the years between
I lost all thoughts of God —
And I never found myself.

In the busy ward
As I come to the end of life,
I find a friend
Who offers mind and heart.
A window opens,
Gently, the God of my fathers
Calls me home.
Now only — I begin.

So I will leave a window.
Who will look though it
And find there
His own starting point?

Cicely Saunders

FRIENDSHIP IN HOSPICE

I watch my friends around me and share their pain.
  I understand their fears.

I know how the illness can wax and wane —
  And sometimes bring tears.

I know the feelings of despair we all must know,
    And sometimes cannot bear.

This is our common bond of friendship,
    As delicate as a hair.

As delicate as the spider's web stretching through the
    trees.
So fine a thread . . .

Liz Selby

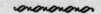

THREE FACES

I did not know any of your names.
A man in his thirties perhaps.
You had a surgical collar about your neck
and a small plastic box on your chest, flashing a red light
for pain control I think.
You were sitting in the hospital bed colouring in a picture.
It seemed to me a strange thing to be doing here.
You told me things were rough
and all I was able to say was 'take it easy'.

The second was a woman with dark eyes
and black curly hair.
I was lying on the treatment couch
wired to drip, wishing I was anywhere but here.

It was all taking, oh so long,
and you, you couldn't stop talking.
You were in pain and frightened, I know
but you just couldn't stop talking.
You said that you felt safe here in the hospital
as if nothing could happen to you.

I was with other cancer patients in a group at the hospice.
There in the corner was a young lad
in his blue dressing gown.
You looked like I did ten years ago . . .
Thin, shy, nervous with glasses. Bewildered.
  Overwhelmed.
I couldn't understand what you were doing here with us.
I thought it was some silly mistake.
I wanted to go over and say something to you
but I didn't know what to say.

The three of you died in three weeks.
You are all dead and I am alive.
And I don't know why.

Paul Harvey

SPASM

Their mouths were moving
But I could not hear their voices.
I felt submerged: suddenly deaf.

I struggled to make sense.
Then I heard them; panic leaving me;
Anxiety hanging on the faces of those around me.
'Shall we touch her?'
'Shall we move her?'
I took control and banished their anxiety with laughter.
My limbs stretched out before me,
Racked, but that torture/punishment not inflicted by
    others.
I watched the muscles ripple and once again felt
    locked inside my body,
Brain and body, rejecting and objecting.
Eternally at odds
The spasm passed and in normal time had not lasted long:
    Ten minutes to eternity.
A lady brought me tea and,
'Never mind dear, you always feel better after one
    of your little turns.'
I could dissolve anxiety round me with tears of laughter,
But my tears could not tumble freely
For mine are trapped.

Ada Cowie

INWARD WEEPING

Inward weeping
    fills me
        from unspoken grief.

Inward weeping —
   sadness lies with
    deep-seated
     agony.

Inward weeping —
   comfort sometimes found
    in quietness
     with someone
      close.

Gwen Rees

I WISH

I wish:

  I were,
    especially gifted;
      a special gift,
the gift of music . . .

I would
  compose
    a serenade
to my wife

Songs of Joy . . .

Fred Julian

VERONICA

What is the use of the cross on the pillow?
  How much does she need it?
    Never did at all.

She was my friend and I loved her.

Only strangers are comforted by symbols . . .
  and such strangers
    and such symbols!

Sometimes we understood each other —
  She more often than I.

When we mutually understood —
  what smiles!
    what grins!
      what happiness!

The bed is empty and flat:
  my friend is gone from here;
    but she is sleeping
      quite near to hand

Soon she will rise
  and smile
    and say 'Good-morning'.

Rita Ford

THE OFFICIAL

He just stared
one of those stares
that deaden all the feelings
that others have warmed.

You'd think they'd be more careful
who they sent.
I mean, we're all fairly damaged
already.

I spoke; he wrote;
Never a 'Good-morning'
or 'How are you?'
If only he could have smiled.

Gwen Rees

SHOCK

Queuing up at the bank
I was feeling watched,
gammy and self conscious;
I was tall.

There was a lot of middle-aged housewives
standing in their flat shoes.
I felt a nudge in my back.
I spun round on my heels — what's up?
This blue-rinsed lady
with her eyebrows on her nose
and her
'I'm-about-to-ask-you-a-big-deep-question' face
 says:
'Why does a young lad like you shave his head?'
'It's not shaved, it fell out.'
She looked at me with a 'why'-face;
she didn't say anything.
Then I said: 'I've got cancer'.
There were no more comments
just a whole row of 'oh-my-god' faces.

Colin Stones

GIRLS

There was Kay
from Golders Green
and several
in between.

Now there's nothing.

Anonymous

JESSIE AND THE DOLL

Elderly lady, dolly-rocking,
Speaking of dreams that are half forgotten.
Holding a doll that you call 'Baby'
Elderly lady, dolly-rocking.

Sweet is the cherry you place on her lips,
So if she should wake she may think it a kiss.
There in your arms like a babe in her cradle —
But only a memory, only a dream.

It's not just a doll that I dress and undress
Fumbling with buttons that fasten her vest.
You just see the silly things, in spite of your kindness
You can't comprehend who I hold to my breast.

For my love is the cherry I touch to her lips
So if she should wake she may know that I'm here.
In my arms lies the child that I stole from the grave
For forty long years she has been in my care.

Elderly lady, dolly-rocking
Whispering dreams — no longer forgotten
Holding a doll that you call 'Baby'
Elderly lady, dolly-rocking.

Sweet is the cherry you placed on her lips
I know when you both wake she'll know it's a kiss.
Rock gently the child lying here in her cradle —
You're joining the memory, becoming the dream.

Jane Eisenhauer

STRANGERS

Scruffy clothes, dirty face
Stale odour hung around her
Pleading sounds filled the room
While around my neck her clammy hands gripped
And with piercing eyes searched for love.

Within my body and my soul I felt complete revulsion
Swiftly the Spirit moved me
Behold this is no stranger here
But the Son of God at last.

Anonymous

RECOVERY

The ups and downs can leave the frowns
Upon your gentle face.
And looking back, along the track
I rush to find the pace
Of love secure that will endure
And be something more than dreaming.

I shudder when I stop and think
How oft your joy was broken.
How deeply felt your stars that melt
And left with just a token
Of what it seemed that you had dreamed.
Where is the point in dreaming?

But you can climb to heights sublime
Up from beneath the surface.
From what seemed rough, with sterner stuff
You rose with fixed purpose.
Of this I'm sure, you can endure
For this world must keep on dreaming.

Tom O'Connor

VISITORS

Through my half-closed eyes,
I see them peeping.
Two little mousey people
Pale, worried and over-awed.
Huddled into worn drab coats.
Apologetically stepping over the threshold,
Whispering, 'sorry dear,
We were looking for Elsie.'
They slip away

[27]

Can it be happening?
Is it closing time?
Purposeful marching –
High-heels and studs thumping.
Loud voices and barely-muffled laughter.
A large group gathers.
Camel-hair coated and crew-cutted men.
Their women bright jumpered,
Gold-trinketted and tinted –
'Ello, luv.
That ain't 'er.
Bit young ain't she?
Watcher!
Tat-tah.
See yer.'

Christine Douglas

FACES

A great responsibility
It is to have a face,
For someone's look may make you free
Or turn you to disgrace.

We are behind our nasty looks;
We cannot see the blows
Of rods in pickle, barbs with hooks,
Or looking down the nose.

But it is best we do not know
Our smiles lit up a day
If ever grace is here to grow
And pride be kept at bay.

Forgetting ours, we look at yours
See peace and joy and love,
And sometimes courage gives us pause
And barriers are moved.

In hospice beds we see them all,
Those looks so full of grace,
Where God has come to make His call
Within a human face.

Cicely Saunders

BUS STOP

The sun is shining.
A slight breeze disturbs
The grit and dust of Mare Street.

There are three of us —
'Wheel-chaired', 'pusher', and 'guide' —
We approach the Bus Stop.

'They' sit on the seats
Swinging their legs,
Laughing and chattering.

Nobody sees us

We are invisible.

'They' huddle in untidy formation
Gazing with blank faces
Waiting with plastic bags.

Transfixed as in a dream world;
Rooted to their piece of pavement,
'They' move neither left nor right.

Our 'guide' steps ahead
To forge a pathway
No word is spoken.

Nobody sees us

We are invisible

Christine Douglas

MORNING AT THE BAZAAR

Doors closed.

Patient patients, bags clutched,
legs covered, purses pinched shut.
Most silent. Waiting, watching; waiting,
Wondering . . . when —

Doors open —

Large, warm
Gulf of sound.
Laughing, greeting, meeting,
clattering, chattering, clamouring

Eyes wide —

blue, green, yellow, orange,
orange, yellow, green, blue, red
lights flashing, colours rushing,
changing, appearing, disappearing
kaleidoscope

Now —

forcing forward, jostling,
bustling, fussing, boisterous,
pushing, jousting
fun!

Fingers tight on the wheels,
crack of the hoops;
the merry-go-round,
the carousels
the fairs.

The prize?
Who cares!

But hands hurt from —
bustling, fussing, boisterous
pushing, jousting
fun!

Quietly retiring
Sedately, sated,
pliant, passive
heading for protection!

Clutching to my bosom
my one bottled
Babycham!

Christine Douglas

THE RAG DOLL

Clarence is a little doll
   Who sits above my bed.
He looks at me with big blue eyes,
   To make sure I'm not dead.

I smile at him each morn I wake,
  He smiles back in return,
We have a friendship, doll and I,
From which there's much to learn.

A name was sought for little doll,
  And Clarence was for choosing.
For he really is a circus clown,
  And it was thought amusing.

His hair is blue and rather straight,
  It suits the clothes he wears,
He has some baggy trousers,
  Which somehow hide the tears.

I love my Clarence very much,
  He's such a friendly bloke.
Sometimes when pain becomes a threat
  My tears he helps to choke.

That's all there is for now, my friends,
  About a man so good.
He sits above me every day
  He's helped me all he could.

John Vollborth

FELLOW TRAVELLERS

Hospice, meeting
        Place of pilgrims;
Trains in station
        Which one's moving?
                Fellow travellers
                Different journeys
                Differing stages
                        Same finale.

Only pilgrims
        Can help pilgrims
Really help them
        Spirits meeting
                Battered travellers
                Bruised and hurting
                Fellow travellers
                        Humbly sharing.

Pilgrim teachers
        Pilgrim learners
Shared advances
        And shared problems
                Always learning
                Always teaching
                Still there's anguish
                        Needing healing.

Growing hope
        For western travellers
Hospice style
        Of patient care
                Needs are vast
                In many countries
                Untold pilgrims
                        Hurting there.

Circle there
       Again evolving
Here and there
       Enthusiasts
            Pilgrim learners
            Patient centred
            Prophet mentors
                 To their peers.

David Frampton

TO THE EDGE

By her bed I was
the hurtful child again.

Virtuous and vicious,
innocence, oblivious,
wounding without will.
Disturbed by my doubt
compelled by conviction
still, waited.

Her bony fingers
fumbled the tousled sheets,
as her dry, lined lips
formed the words that came
in stuttered whisper —
'doctor — will I die?'

Her brief, brittle gaze
stifling fury, amidst fear,
pleading pride, from indignity,
walked us to the edge of hope
and stood us on the precipice
of understanding.

I took her hand, and she
read as a blind man braille.
I said enough and
together we stepped out.

The anguish acknowledged
her scalding sorrow flowed,
and she wept.
No reassurance but release;
no comfort but confidence;
an affirmation of trust;
an absolution of truth.

As I leave, my feet
heavier on the floor,
the child is a man again;
always older, and sighing
in sad speculation.

When must that man measure
his own mortality?
For how long will he walk
willingly
                    to the edge?

Kilian Dunphy

REMINISCENCE THERAPY

And what did Mary remember?
Children bright and hungry as birds,
Hands knobby with cold, noses running,
Spinning like tops in grimy streets.

Then the old woman remembered
Rolling up in warmth; her marriage bed;
Youth and passion – the springing days
When blood leapt quick and sweet.

What next, Mary, what came after?
Womb-weary, wretched, swollen days.
Nurse, what do you know of our hard times?
Children were born one way or another.

Alone Mary dreamed her dream
Bleached, shrivelled, all juices sucked out.
Give me a strong man again, sweet flesh
To water my barren parts.

Like a blown leaf on a pillow drift
She dies an ordinary death.
But I remember my sister's life
And lay her out with a special care.

Anna Brown

TO PAM FROM A YOUNG DOCTOR

I wanted to talk to her of death,
and knew nothing of it
but the textbook pain that
I had read and learnt about
and read the fear in her
staring eyes, now too
large for her still recognisable head.

So I about faced
and tried to raid my memories
but foolishly talked of futures —
mine not hers —
futile irrelevancies.
Until almost plucking
from the thin air
that she expired
said 'I'm sorry,
I love you so,'
and she took my hand.

Now I begin to understand.

John Smith

I IMAGINE . . .

I imagine you've travelled thousands of miles
   to find a secret place.
Your maps have been burnt and the weather is shaping
   the lines upon your face.
The days have been lost in living a dream
   and your work has turned to sweat.
The sensations build up an echo to tell you
   you haven't finished yet.
And striding forward without a thought
   for the legs that carry you on,
You suddenly stumble and fracture the plan,
   from which your life has shone.
You taste the dust on which you walked
   and feel your tongue is dry,
And the future freezes, shrinks and dies
   as clouds of time float by.
And as you lie with many thoughts
   a child may find you there;
He stands above you, speaks in tongues
   and gently strokes your hair.
The eyes of the child rest upon you,
   he'll help you all he can;
Like this, a doctor (mildly short-sighted)
   tends a dying man.

Peter Kaye

OPPOSITE VIEWS

I have tried hard these days
    to understand how it is
    for you
To put myself inside
    of you
and see from the inside
    how it is.

Not physically I mean.
That I can imagine well enough.
    The frustration
    The impotence
    The pain
    The indignity
of not being able to do for yourself
what we so carelessly
take for granted.

The having to bear
the clumsy attempts
    of well meaning people
who want to help
but do not know if they should,
or if you need it
or if you want it.

The having to bear the endless talk
    of old men
without being one:
the talk of Hopkins
    when perhaps you hate to hear
    about springs and sunsets which
you cannot see.

The talk of pious retreatants
who walk with downcast eyes
and seem so full of God
when He is so far away.

I long to know
    what I have no right to know.
But I want to know
    because I care about you.
I am curious because
    I love you.

Sheila Cassidy

MY GIFT

Handle me with care.
The wrapper's worn
and held by threadbare string,
almost torn apart;
gaping edges
invite you to look with curious eyes.
Worthless, you might think.
So old, carelessly parcelled up.

Just think before you touch
think where I have been,
seen, spoken, listened, touched,

hurt, born and felt.
Can't you feel the passion
left within me?

Share it,
undo the string, slowly please.
(I'm so slow now)
undo the hurt
(I hurt now)
the guilt
(aren't you guilty too?)
the hate
(as I hate what's happening now)
undo the love
      and let it go,
            my gift to you.

John Smith

⌇⌇⌇⌇⌇

IF WHEELCHAIRS
WERE A PRAM

In wheels I sit
and steer myself around,
thinking it was wheels
that I began
to travel first
down bumpy paths;
to lie beneath the trees

and sleep,
or wonder at
the movement of the leaves.

Pram-bound explorer's feet
have never felt
the ground their wheels compress.
I wish paralysis
brought with it innocence.
I weep because I know
what lies beyond the fence
where dead legs will not go.

If wheelchairs were a pram
then I could throw a toy or rattle
crashing to the ground
to ease my rage.
I would know
but they would laugh
not blame
thinking it was
just a baby's game.

Babies cannot speak
as I can.
Nor can they recall
Christmases or courting.
Is speech a gain
when every word is sad?
Memory
increases grief for me.
Return me to my pram.

Averil Stedeford

NEW WHEELS

A very private man
he came through grief
when someone dared to spring
the trap of solitude,
a trundling cart, rattling bin
to early execution.

New wheels he bought,
ingeniously controlled,
a wheelchair so responsive
to his touch
that he could take it almost anywhere.

The greying engineer
took much delight
in this invention:
new technology, as
canny as himself.

Down the village street he rode
with steady speed, over the curb
and into the village shop
to buy his baccy,
wink at girls,
and talk about the cricket.

For six good weeks
he travelled cheerfully
grumbled a bit but
was a man again.

His last wheels were the hearse
that took him down
the old familiar street.

The curse of death
had lifted wheels before.
Only his useless body went
out through the chapel door.

Averil Stedeford

BEGINNINGS

Last night Miss Palmer died.
Some of us cried
But as it was carols
Most of us went on with the singing.
I couldn't decide
If this was the end, or the beginning

Then it was past midnight —
Turn off the light
And your face to the wall.
I suppose this is Christmas dawning?
It doesn't seem right
That we should be glad in the morning.

Yet, today He was born
Nor did He scorn
A humble beginning;
Nor a humble life nor a humble end.
And so on this morn
We must try to be glad with our friend.

So I tried, as I drove
To see His love
At work in the world –
They die harder elsewhere
But something did move: –
For the first time I found He was there.

Anonymous

⟋⟍⟋⟍⟋⟍⟋⟍

STEPPING OUT

I believe that God
has the whole World
in his hands.
He is not a bystander
at the pain of the World.
He does not stand
like Peter,
wringing his hands
in the shadow
but is there
in the dock
on the rack
high on the gallow-tree.
He is in the pain
of the lunatic,
the tortured,
those racked by grief.

His is the blood
that flows in the gutter.
His are the veins
burned by heroin.
His the lungs
choked by AIDS.
His is the heart
broken and suffering.
His the despair
of the mute,
the oppressed.

Bow down in awe
before the paradox.
Before the mystery
of God made man.
Search and you will find
but you will not understand.
You must learn to live
to laugh
to love
baffled and bemused.

You must learn to walk
in the dark,
on the water
towards a voice,
a star,
a hand outstretched.

But you must get out of the boat.

Sheila Cassidy

NIGHT SKY

The day sky is still and high
With trees and clouds or jumbo planes
Across it.

But the night sky moves.

The day sky can be assumed;
A wash for shirts and sheets
And smalls.

But O the night sky is huge.

Birds fly through the day sky
And the sun rises
And then the rain falls.

But the night sky broods.

The day sky is thin and safe
Earth wheels and wonders
Under it.

But the night sky is full of fears
And deep, and pin-points
The stars.

Tom West

EMBER DAYS

Ember Days are days,
when the heart grows warmer.
When memories sweet,
and love complete,
Make the heart grow calmer

We consider the kindness
of loved one and friend
And remember the joy
of a love without end

....

It's nice to read of lovely things —
of making words and nether rings

Like using Ember days
to make the heart grow warm

And oh how gentle it can be
to see the fading day
in ember shades

....

I sit with the light dimmed,

the flames die down.

Sitting all alone,
dreaming of the past.

Seeing shadow figures
in the dying embers.

Poetry group

DAD YOU DIDN'T TELL ME

'Hi! Dad' I used to say, as I walked through the door,
'Are you feeling better than you did before?
You look a little brighter, what did the doctor say?
Dad you didn't tell me that you were going away.'

'I am feeling fine,' you said, 'and the pain is not so bad.
I'll go and see about it if you promise not to nag.'
'There's no need to worry,' I've often heard you say,
Dad you didn't tell me that you were going away.

You must have known for some time and kept it to
yourself,

If only you had told me, I might have been some help.
A proud and independent man, what more is there to say,
Dad you didn't tell me that you were going away.

Eileen Tompkins

SO ANGRY

I would like to say
I think you have been away long enough.
Yes!
I most definitely would like to say
categorically
that you have been away long enough.

Also, that you went
without a proper goodbye.
Now,
I know that was not your fault,
beyond your control,
still,
I feel I have cause for complaint.

I am angry with you
so angry.
My insides are knotted so tightly
only a knife could cut through to my pain.
Didn't I tell you to think differently?

Didn't I say,
'tell your body what to do,
don't allow it to dictate to you?'

But you wouldn't listen.
You didn't listen.
If you were here with me now
I would make you listen.
You've gone away
I am alone.
I have no one to share things with.
How could you do that to me?

I would like to say,
categorically,
that you have been away long enough,
long enough.

Grace Smith

FEELINGS

Let me tell you this my friend,
  The things you feel today,
The hurt and the unhappiness,
  It seems won't go away.

They sometimes slip out of mind,
   For a moment or even two,
But, then they creep up on you,
   When you least expect them to.

These feelings that you feel, my friend,
   It sometimes helps to tell,
For I have felt them too, my friend,
   So I know these feelings well.

The feelings that you have, my friend,
   Don't be afraid to let them show,
For these only come to you, my friend,
   For someone you love so.

Mary Chitty

MEMORIES

You can never lose someone you love,
   Not like a purse or a ring.
Just because you can no longer see them —
   That doesn't mean a thing.

You can never lose someone you love,
    Not like a watch or a chain.
As long as the love's in your heart,
    The memories will always remain.

Mary Chitty

WINGS

Look high and see the swift,
dark and sickle,
cutting a swath across the sky
of my horizon.

This traveller has flown
inspired paths
Leading from all it loved, and left
to visit me.

She knows the hard red earth
and the hard sky,
has skimmed the great grey naked rocks
I had to climb.

(I cannot bear the throb
of village drums
beating beneath a man's black hand
on my memory)

Oh rest and nest for now
in my house;
Folding your wings and hatching your young
under the eaves —

Though when your young are grown
and hear the cry
that Africa sends out to these she owns
I'll be bereft.

But no!
The empty shells are here.
My heart has flown
borne on swift wings across the sky
To those I love.

Tom West

THE LAST FAREWELL

An ocean liner moves
 dark against the dawn.

A barefoot woman
 in blue chiffon
  watches from the shore.

Tears fall against her cheek.
This is goodbye,
the last farewell.

Sunrise — soft gold,
colouring the sky,
but not yet lightening

This last goodbye.

Gwen Rees

THE FATHER

They watched him through each stroke,
drowning slightly every time.
Discouraged by ineptitude or platitude
He realised that the coast-line was receding.

At first they swam, almost alongside
But gradually too far out
He could not know
if he was being recalled
or begged to stay away.

Perhaps there was collusion
in the muted cries.
Words lost in the wind
of flat despair
blowing them inexorably apart.

Only now while the sea is calm
　　And the storm a year away
　　　　Is there a new desire to call him back
Now, useless, the words are stronger than before.

Jane Eisenhauer

THE HEAVY STONE

My grief was a heavy stone,
rough and sharp.
Grasping to pick it up
my hands were cut.

Afraid to let it go
I carried it.
While I had my grief
you were not lost.

The rain of my tears
smoothed it.
The wind of my rage
weathered it,
making it round and small.

The cuts in my hands have healed.
Now in my palm it rests,
sometimes almost beautiful,
sometime almost of you.

Averil Stedeford

SOUNDS FROM THE MIDDLE FLOOR

Over the roar of Mare Street
a bird sits high and sings.

The darkness hides his plumage
but not the dawn his wings.

He sees the coming daylight;
the new-made hope of day.

Sing bird! Sing!
What is singing
but to pray?

Your voice among the rooftops
in dark and icy days
is promise of God's tryst —
That Spring will come with praise.

Rita Ford

TO 'SUNSHINE'

He's only a bird in a wicker cage
But he's meant so much to me:
So small and yellow with plumage so bright,
A real delight to see.

One night when my spirits were very low,
And tears were dimming my eyes,
He started to sing in a voice so pure,
It took me by surprise.

Such a paean of sound from the tiny throat,
A song of joy and praise;
And he seemed to repeat again and again
Two notes at the start of each phrase.

'Come on, come on' and again 'Come on,
Listen to what I say.
Think of the happiness you have had
And the beauty of each new day.'

'There's still such a lot for you to do,
You can find so much to give;
Perhaps you can help another soul
To find the will to live.'

'If I can sing in my wicker cage,
Shut in day after day,
Surely you with the freedom you have,
Can open your heart and say,

"Take my life, O Lord my God,
That I may ever be
Used in any way you wish,
Always, Lord, for Thee".'

Dorothy Newton

MOURN NO MORE

Mourn no more; she's left us for
The deep and dappled woodland
Where fox and badger, secretly,
Her progress contemplate
And the darting blackbird's cries
Arouse in her desire.

No longer weep; her journey's on.
The heather scented moorland
Where grazing ewes, sad faced,
Her purposes enquire,
While the loose-winged, mewing buzzards
Coax her into flight.

Mourn no more; she's climbing
To the lone mysterious mountain,
Beyond whose crags the tumbling ravens
Greet the upward surge,
And the whispering wind alone
Knows her intent.

Neil Gadsby

Index of 'Authors'

Index of First Lines
and Titles